AGGIE
GOES TO AFRICA

AGGIE
GOES TO AFRICA

MIKE PAVELKA

Library of Congress Control Number: 2024921333

ISBN: 979-8-89228-245-1   (Paperback)
ISBN: 979-8-89228-246-8   (eBook)

Book Ordering Information:
Atticus Publishing
548 Market St PMB 70756
San Francisco, CA 94104
(888) 208-9296
info@atticuspublishing.com
www.atticuspublishing.com

Printed in the United States of America

Table of Contents

Introduction

In April of 1996 the company had a second quarter meeting where it was announced that the field I took care of in North Louisiana would be sold and I would be terminated. I began looking for a new job and I was told about a job overseas in West Africa. I met with the in-country manager and went for the job. After a series of interviews, I was selected and went there as the engineering manager of a facility that produced +/- 3500 bbls of 65 degree condensate, 45 mmcf/d of gas from a monobore platform out of one well alba #2 into a 10" pipeline that carried it to a production facility called a harp as it looked like a string harp with two 10" vertical pipes with the ground to the 4 sets of pipes perpendicular to those pipes sloping to the back and bottom of the harp where the water (minimum interstitial produced water off the tite reservoir sandstone (16 md was the permeability) dropped out was collected and sent to the flare. The oil was sent to the 50,000 bbl bolted tanks. The gas came out of the top of the harp and was sent thru the separator with a Joules Thompson valve to drop the temperature to -32 degrees f and cause the oil to separate and be sent to the stock tanks where it warmed up the vapor off the tanks came out with a dangerous side effect of catching fire by a stray bullet or campfire (two subjects that will be discussed later).

On August 1, 1996, I landed in Malabo. Poverty cannot be explained in enough terms to make it understandable. I had been to Mexico, but that was nowhere near the degree of problems I saw in Malabo. A family of six survived on \$32/month. The wife, possibly up to five, managed everything —working on the farm, caring for the home, the children, the husband, the elders, and the sick. They also ran a small grocery business (simple grocery items) and handled the finances with skill. The education of the people was non-existent the educated ones had been to Russia, Spain, China, and the USA. Those educated in China seemed better educated than those in Spain, Russia, or the USA. It seemed Russia's focus was on educating them for future exploitation —whether for gold, timber, ivory, or food —while the people were left without the help they needed. The political people (ambassadors) from the countries wanted to try to change the politics of this nation instead of helping the people with health, farming, roads and water, electricity, housing, and sanitation. Nobody wanted to act because of the rampant corruption. They kept pushing us to take action, but with only four American expats, it was tough. Many didn't help much and tried to pass off their responsibilities when they went on vacation. Meanwhile, in Houston, there was no coordination. Projects like the propane or mosquito initiatives were left hanging if someone went on vacation, with no one stepping in to keep things going.

Weather in My New Place

Malabo, the capital of Equatorial Guinea, has a tropical monsoon climate (termed Köppen Am). It is located on the island of Bioko in the Gulf of Guinea and is characterized by high temperatures, high humidity, and heavy rainfall.

The average annual temperature in Malabo is 26.4°C (79.5°F), with very little variation throughout the year. The warmest months are February and March, with average temperatures of 27.5°C and 27.6°C (81.5°F and 81.7°F), respectively. The coolest months are August and September, with average temperatures of 25.4°C (77.7°F).

Malabo receives an average of 1,850 millimeters (73 inches) of rain per year. The city has a pronounced, albeit short, sunnier (but still cloudy) dry season from December through February. January is normally its driest month with 29 millimeters (1.14

inches) of rain falling on average. It also has a very long cloudy wet season that covers the remaining nine months from March to November. On average, the months hit hardest by the wet season are September and October, which receive 500 millimeters (20 inches) of rain and showers between them.

The humidity in Malabo is high year-round, averaging around 80%. This can make the city feel quite uncomfortable, especially during the wet season.

The wind in Malabo is generally light to moderate, with the strongest winds occurring during the dry season. The prevailing wind direction is southwest.

Overall, the climate of Malabo is hot, humid, and rainy. Visitors should pack light, breathable clothing, an umbrella, and sunscreen.

My daughter Bamboo and the chimp Lucy playing in Malabo

UNDERSTANDING AFRICA

કે • ક

Africa, a vast and diverse continent, has undergone remarkable changes over the past few decades. The stark contrast between Africa in the 1990s and Africa today reflects a story of resilience, development, and progress.

In the 1990s, Africa grappled with countless challenges. Political instability, economic crises, and social unrest were widespread. The HIV/AIDS epidemic ravaged communities, claiming millions of lives. Poverty was widespread, and many struggled to access basic education and healthcare. Civil wars and conflicts tore through several regions, causing immense suffering and displacing countless people.

Fast forward to today, Africa presents a different picture. Economic growth has been significant, with many countries experiencing rapid industrialization and infrastructural development. Foreign direct investment has poured into the continent, fostering innovation and creating job opportunities. The emergence of a vibrant middle class has contributed to a thriving consumer market.

One of the most notable transformations has been in the realm of technology. Africa has leapfrogged traditional development stages and embraced cutting-edge technology. Mobile phone penetration is widespread, providing access to communication and services even in remote areas. The rise of fintech has transformed banking, bringing financial services within reach for more people than ever before. Moreover, Africa has become a hub for tech startups, fostering entrepreneurship and innovation.

In terms of healthcare, significant strides have been made in the fight against diseases like malaria, tuberculosis, and HIV/AIDS. Increased access to antiretroviral therapy has significantly reduced mortality rates. International partnerships and investments have bolstered healthcare infrastructure, improving the quality of services across the continent.

Education has also seen improvements. Efforts have been made to enhance school enrollment and literacy rates. Access to quality education has expanded, empowering a new generation with the knowledge and skills necessary for a rapidly evolving global economy.

Despite the progress, challenges persist. Issues such as political instability, corruption, and inequality still need to be addressed. Climate change threatens many African nations, causing environmental degradation and disrupting agriculture.

Africa's journey from the 1990s to today showcases the continent's resilience and unwavering determination. While there is still work to be done, the transformation witnessed over the past few decades serves as a beacon of hope, inspiring further efforts towards a prosperous and sustainable future for all African nations.

Political Landscape in Africa

The political landscape in Africa is a tapestry of diverse ideologies, governments, and social structures. While there have been remarkable advancements in democratization processes across the continent, challenges persist, profoundly impacting society. One such incident that exemplifies the emotional toll of political unrest occurred in Nigeria during the #EndSARS protests in October 2020.

In many African nations, political instability, corruption, and poor governance have led to widespread disillusionment among citizens. Africa's history is marked by colonialism, leading to the emergence of complex political systems. Post-independence, numerous countries struggled to establish stable governments, often marred by coups and authoritarian regimes. While strides toward democratic governance have been made, instances of electoral fraud, human rights violations, and lack of political transparency remain concerns.

Political Unrest

Beyond isolated incidents, the persistent political challenges in Africa have far-reaching consequences. Trust in institutions erodes, leading to a sense of disillusionment and apathy among citizens. Economic growth is impeded as political instability often deters foreign investments. Additionally, the lack of effective governance hampers social development initiatives, impacting education, healthcare, and infrastructure.

Furthermore, political unrest frequently exacerbates social divisions, leading to ethnic or religious tensions. In some cases, these tensions escalate into violent conflicts, displacing communities and disrupting social cohesion. The emotional trauma of such events lingers for years, affecting the mental well-being of those involved.

Addressing the political challenges in Africa requires a concerted effort from governments, civil society, and the international community. Strengthening democratic institutions, ensuring transparency in governance, and upholding the rule of law are essential steps. Investments in education and awareness programs can empower citizens to actively engage in politics, fostering a sense of ownership and accountability.

In conclusion, the political situation in Africa, marked by both progress and challenges, profoundly impacts society. The emotional incidents, such as the #EndSARS protests, serve as stark reminders of the human cost of political unrest. By fostering stability, unity, and democratic values, African nations can pave the way for a brighter, more equitable future for their citizens.

Bridging the Gap in Africa

Africa, a continent of rich cultural diversity and abundant natural resources, stands in stark contrast to Europe in terms of development. While Europe boasts advanced economies, robust infrastructures, and high standards of living; Africa, despite its potential, grapples with underdevelopment and lags behind many other regions. Several factors contribute to this disparity, highlighting the need for focused efforts to bridge the gap between these two continents.

A significant factor shaping Africa's current developmental challenges is its history of colonization. European powers colonized vast parts of Africa, exploiting resources and disrupting indigenous social structures. The legacy of colonialism left African nations with fragmented economies, divisive borders, and a legacy of inequality. In contrast, many European nations experienced industrial revolutions, leading to rapid economic growth, technological advancements, and the establishment of stable institutions.

Economic Disparities

Europe boasts some of the world's largest economies, characterized by diverse sectors, including manufacturing, finance, and technology. Countries like Germany, France, and the United Kingdom are global economic powerhouses, contributing significantly to the world's GDP. In contrast, many African nations struggle with low GDP per capita, limited industrialization, and dependency on agriculture. The lack of access to capital, skilled labor, and technology hamper Africa's ability to compete on the global stage.

Infrastructure and Access to Basic Services

Europe's well-developed infrastructure includes extensive road networks, efficient public transportation systems, and advanced telecommunication services. In contrast, Africa faces significant challenges in infrastructure development. Limited access to electricity, inadequate transportation networks, and insufficient healthcare facilities hinder socioeconomic progress. The lack of reliable infrastructure affects education, healthcare, and overall quality of life for millions of Africans.

Education and Human Capital Development

Europe invests heavily in education, fostering a skilled workforce equipped to thrive in the global knowledge economy. Many European countries offer free or affordable education, ensuring high literacy rates and advanced skill sets among their citizens. In contrast, Africa struggles with disparities in education quality and access. Limited resources, outdated curricula, and social barriers impede educational opportunities for millions of children, affecting their prospects and the continent's overall development.

Healthcare Disparities and Disease Burden

Europe boasts advanced healthcare systems with universal access to medical services, cutting-edge research, and comprehensive public health initiatives. In contrast, Africa faces substantial healthcare challenges, including high maternal and child mortality rates, prevalent infectious diseases such as malaria and HIV/AIDS, and limited access to essential healthcare services. These challenges strain healthcare infrastructures and hinder progress in improving overall public health.

Addressing the Disparities: A Path to Progress

Addressing Africa's developmental disparities requires comprehensive strategies and global cooperation. Investments in education, healthcare, and infrastructure are crucial to building a foundation for sustainable development. International partnerships can facilitate technology transfer, knowledge exchange, and skill development, empowering African nations to harness their potential fully.

Moreover, promoting good governance, combating corruption, and ensuring political stability are essential for creating an environment conducive to economic growth and social progress. Empowering women, addressing social inequalities, and promoting entrepreneurship can further drive innovation and economic diversification.

The developmental gap between Africa and Europe is a multifaceted challenge rooted in historical, economic, and social factors. While progress has been made in various African countries, sustained efforts, both domestically and internationally, are necessary to uplift the continent. By addressing these disparities and fostering inclusive, sustainable development, Africa can emerge as a global economic force, ensuring a better future for its people and contributing significantly to the global community.

LEAVING THE USA
THE DATE IS AUGUST 30, 1992

I boarded American Airlines with four pieces of luggage for Miami, then on to Madrid, Spain.

The flight was coach because the company was saving money and a group of employees believed I would not be there for a month. I arrived in Miami and found Iberia Airlines, and got checked in. Again, I boarded the flight and flew to Madrid. And since the flight flew from Houston to Malabo, I didn't worry about the luggage. I went to the hotel, bathed, and watched the USA's first pro-NBA players in the Olympics – very fascinating. I remember watching Mr. Charles Barkley look over his left shoulder and then pass the ball behind his back to the baseline, which caused the referee to jump out of the way—he thought he was going to be hit. But it hit inbounds at his feet, and with the spin Sir Charles had put on, it bounded up in the hands of the center and was dunked for 2 points. The crowd went wild, but this was only the start of the schooling for the tournament. There were many fascinating highlights in the game, but due to jet lag and the coming day, I fell asleep.

The next morning, I awoke for a breakfast buffet and the start of my travel adventures to Malabo.

When I got to the airport, I got checked in, but that was the only part that would be simple and easy.

I found my luggage was not checked in as this was not part of the airplane deal like I was told. So, I had to find it and recheck it to Malabo, which cost $1600 – I was not a happy camper, but I boarded the flight, and we were off to the Canary Islands. The landing was nice, but it was night, and they refueled the plane, and we were off for Dakar, Senegal. We landed at Dakar Senegal Airport, about a half mile from the airport, on the tarmac in the night heat of the Sahara Desert with the heavy smell of camel dung in the air, which didn't compare to the odor of the unairconditioned smell of the airport where the bathroom had not been cleaned in a few years, or a honey truck had emptied the latrine. We stayed in the first setting room for about an hour. Then we moved thru the gift shop, which was neither lit nor airconditioned. I was scared because they were going to easily arrest me for theft since everything in the gift shop could be taken easily or claimed you had taken it, but I made it into the next waiting area, which was airconditioned. We waited there and then proceeded back across the tarmac to the aircraft, where we reboarded and took off for Malabo. Well, finally I could go to my actual destination.

I don't remember how long it took before we landed, but there was an Equatorial Guinea military man in a seat one row up and to my right. There were lots of passengers speaking to him, and for some, he would stand up, and for others, he would not. His hat had his name, but when I tried to look at it, he flipped it over, so I gave him my business card and tried to introduce myself, which didn't sit too well. But I made a note of it for future reference.

MAMBOSON WELCOME (FANG)

We landed at Malabo International Airport, which had a lot of broken and damaged aircraft with lots of green vegetation all around the airport, giving a surreal and somewhat eerie ambiance to the entire scene. It was certainly a unique sight that highlighted the airport's need for maintenance and upkeep.

The plane stopped on the tarmac, and we deplaned down the stairs. I was introduced to the interpreter, and we went into the airport, which would be called the chicken coup by its size, and the passport control was behind the chicken wire in a cage.

As soon as I got my luggage, it had to be opened and go through, but since I had locks on it all and limited them to one piece at a time, which didn't sit too well with them, they didn't get to take anything. After this, we got in the truck and rode through the jungle to the camp. The truck driver helped me with my luggage. I went into the mess hall to meet the chef, who was from Lebanon and a good person – we still talk on Facebook. I got settled in and had my first meal, which was chicken, and it was very tasty, like a symphony of flavors dancing on my taste buds, enticing my senses with each succulent bite. However, I was so tired and jet-lagged that I didn't know what was up or down.

The world around me felt like a topsy-turvy whirlwind, leaving me disoriented and unsure of my own orientation. I had many others to meet, so I walked around the area, introducing myself and being introduced to others. After a long two days, I had had it and hit the bed in my place. But the sleep I had hoped for wasn't all as quiet as I hoped due to scratching on the ceiling. Restless and fatigued, I tossed and turned, my mind preoccupied with the mysterious sounds. Was it a mischievous rodent or an unexpected plumbing issue? I would never know, but I yearned for peaceful slumber, yet the incessant scratching echoed through the night.

GOOD MORNING AMBOLA (FANG)

My following days were spent learning about people and the equipment. Since I had worked in the oil field for 25 years, I had a basic understanding of most of the equipment and its processing and operations. The oil, gas, and water as it came in from the offshore platform would enter through a 10" pipeline, then go into the harp, which was two lines perpendicular to the other lines and four lines coming off two perpendicular lines, which are stacked on top of the bottom four lines. The magic was the stainless line running from the front of the harp to the rear of the harp, which allowed pressure equalizing of the gas, oil (condensate), and water (produced water and glycol) to separate the gas flowed out of the top pipe on the back of the harp. In contrast, the oil came out of the middle of the harp, and water was discharged from the bottom of the harp. This process was successfully used in other places, so it was decided to implement it in Malabo.

The gas is taken out of the top of the front of the harp and sent to the separator, which is where the gas goes through a JT valve (Joules Thompson), which, due to the pressure drop, made the gas temperature drop to minus 32 degrees Fahrenheit. The oil was then sent to the 50,000-barrel oil stock tanks. The tanks were bolted. And since they were bolted, they sprung leaks as the seams where the bolts were would expand and contract with the change of the oil temperature and the atmospheric temperature.

Since this is a common issue in our industry, our staff had the required training to deal with such issues. They used the best possible solution to ensure that the company profits remained high with the least loss of precious petroleum products.

Our workers would loosen the bolts and stick stripping in there until the leak was plugged and then tighten the nuts and bolt back tight. Since the tanks were heating up, the vapors would come out of the tanks, and as this is very flammable, it was not good to have a fire or hot objects near the fumes. When we found the military guards cooking in the area, we asked them to stop to prevent a fire or explosion. But we were told that they needed to chop (eat). And since they had AK-47s and we had none, we drove to the ministry, where we explained to them the danger of cooking near the tanks. But they agreed with the soldiers until we explained about the fire causing an explosion. It was surely a dangerous situation. Then we all got in our vehicle and went out, where the ministry explained to the military about not cooking near the tanks – problem solved for a short amount of time.

A short time later, another version of this problem would surface again. Malabo always continued to throw surprises at us.

WORK
ESIEN (FANG)

$\approx \bullet \ll$

The people who worked with us were very proud of their work. Since most of them were kin to the government people, they would try their best, and since most were former carpenters or structural building workers with concrete, their oilfield technical knowledge was limited. So, training was constantly required. We recognized the value of investing time and resources into helping them with the necessary skills and knowledge. Our team understood that their commitment and eagerness to learn outweighed any initial limitations they faced. So, we dedicated ourselves to providing continuous training sessions to enhance their technical expertise and their understanding of the oilfield industry.

While there were good and bad students, there were also good and bad teachers, and I learned about the favorite tree technique that has helped me in many ways since then. When things didn't go well, rather than lose my temper and make wrong decisions, I would go to a tree and discuss with the tree. Most of the time, it would get religious with lots of cussing and description of the failure to perform and how the failure happened and why it occurred and how it shouldn't have happened and hopefully couldn't happen again, but surely, there would be another version but hopefully without the same degree of failure.

In the shade of those wise branches, I found solace and a strange sense of understanding. The tree, standing tall and unyielding, became my confidant. Its silence spoke volumes, and as I poured out my frustrations, I often found clarity in the midst of chaos. The rustling leaves whispered secrets of resilience, and the sturdy trunk seemed to symbolize unwavering strength. Over time, my tree conversations evolved from venting sessions to moments of introspection. I learned to reflect on my actions, dissect my failures, and plan for a better future. Each visit to my favorite tree became a therapeutic journey, and through this unconventional dialogue, I discovered a newfound resilience within myself.

This unconventional coping mechanism not only kept me grounded but also helped me make better decisions in times of frustration. I learned that sometimes, the best answers come from within, and all it takes is a quiet moment with a trusted companion, even if that companion is a tree.

HELLO (FRIEND)
AMBOLA VWING

The days were long and with rain (not a monsoon) and heat from the long pants and long-sleeved shirts. The long pants and shirt and long sleeves were to keep the bugs, flies, and mosquitoes from biting as much as possible, which brought malaria and dengue fever, plus other problems like mango flies. These problems were specific to regions like Africa, and most of the people coming from developed countries were not naturally prepared for these health issues. Keeping sanitized laundry was an essential requirement to work in Malabo for a continuous period, so the company brought the required utilities and services for the comfort of its staff members.

Our clothes were washed in regular USA washing machines and dried in driers brought in from the USA (repair of these machines was not easy as no spare parts were available, so ordering parts from the USA and brought on a ship after being boxed and shipped was not easy). The laundry routine, though cumbersome, symbolized our commitment to frugality. We learned to repair these machines with resourcefulness, as spare parts were scarce. Ordering and shipping parts from the USA involved complex logistics, but we persevered. This mirrored our overall mission to optimize every aspect of our operation. We needed to keep things running with our resourcefulness, as otherwise, life would become quite challenging.

We were challenged to cut costs, but the process of education in Houston was not easy. In Houston, education presented its own challenges. Navigating a foreign education system demanded resilience, but it also broadened our horizons. Each obstacle, from laundry repairs to educational pursuits, taught us valuable lessons about adaptability and determination. We washed the clothes, then dried them, and then they were ironed – why, because of the mango flies. There were many problems associated with clothes. If the clothes were dried outside, the mango flies would lay rice-shaped eggs, which need to be ironed to kill the eggs. Otherwise, the eggs would get under the skin, where a worm would hatch and need a hole above it for air. To get rid of the worm, place Vaseline over the hole. And when the worm needed air, it would push its head up for a breath of air, so with tweezers, you grabbed its head and pulled it out. Otherwise, squeezing it may bust it under the skin, which may cause infection. We had around 40 employees plus the few with the drilling operation.

These peculiar rituals of clothing care became a vital part of our daily routine, a defense against nature's unexpected challenges. Ironing clothes, an ordinary chore back home, became a safeguard against potential health risks. Our adaptability shone through in these moments. We learned to coexist with the environment, even its smallest inhabitants. We found solutions for everything that life threw at us in Malabo. It was a testament to our resourcefulness, turning mundane tasks into life-saving practices. These experiences taught us not only about hygiene but also resilience in the face of the unknown.

We had around 40 employees plus the few with the drilling operation. There was one on the rig and one onshore who stayed at the staff house in Malabo and drove a white vehicle and knew a bunch of the important people as he had been there several months, so he was a good source of information as to who would help us and just wanted something. You needed connections if you wanted anything in that area. The resources were limited, and you needed direct access like they had in Malabo. Otherwise, it was hard to find stuff in the country. However, everything became available if you were friends with the 'right' people, the powerful ones in the city.

We made our first trip to the platform where the drilling rig was set, although when they had moved on, they had broken one of the Kevlar cables to keep the platform standing up when the rig was not there. The rig was drilling Alba no. 3 to below 10,000 feet md. through the isonga gas-condensate sand. The original well, Alba no. 1, was originally discovered by Repsol (a Spanish oil co.) but plugged and abandoned as the World Bank wanted the gas to be reinjected so the gas would not just be flared. The gas-oil ratio was 60-70 bbls/mmcf (remember the JT effect). It basically made the economics of the project non-economical, so Repsol plugged and abandoned the well. Then our company made a deal with the government and the World Bank to produce the well and, along with LPG production plus a methanol plant to turn the gas into methanol and LNG to be sold. This collaboration marked a pivotal moment, merging industry, government, and international support to harness the region's resources for economic growth and sustainability. The ambitious project not only aimed to extract valuable resources but also to utilize them efficiently, ensuring a multi-faceted approach to development. It exemplified our commitment to responsible resource management, economic progress, and environmental stewardship on a global scale.

After the Alba no. 3 well on the rig was completed, and the broken Kevlar cable was fixed, they moved to another exploration well closer to Cameroon (which means shrimp in Portuguese). So, the story goes: the Portuguese landed on the beach and met a fellow walking along the beach and asked him what was the name of this place. Since the native didn't speak Portuguese, he held up his bucket, and the Portuguese didn't speak Fang, and since it had shrimp in the bucket, the Portuguese said the name was Cameroon. And that was how the country got its name. We see this type of story play out all around the world in different regions. The story of the name Kangaroo in Australia is similar to this naming scheme.

Let's get back to our oil well now. It was near the lines of the three countries, Equatorial Guinea, Cameroon, and Nigeria. And since the 800-pound gorilla was Nigeria, they buzzed the rig, and a jet flying over your head is quite loud in the open ocean where the vastness accentuates the roar of its engines, echoing across the endless expanse of water. This was a problem we certainly couldn't tackle. Since this was above my pay grade, we let Houston handle it, and since the well was dry and plugged, it was a moot point.

During the time they were drilling the exploration well, we went back to the Alba platform, and we could see the fog on the platform. I went up there, and they asked why I didn't want help. At this point, I said, "If something goes wrong, I want you fishing for me." So, I swung on the platform landing, which had two ropes – one small blue one and a larger white one. I would use the smaller one to wait for the boat to back up to the landing and the wave to be at maximum height, then I would grab the white rope and swing onto the landing where I would go up the ladder to the manway, shut it, and then go up the choke and shut the well-in and then get help up there. Since the x-mas trees were hot, it took several minutes to bleed off the pressure and knock the choke down and apart, then change the packing, put everything back together, and run a small stainless steel tubing between the crown valve of the tree (Alba #2&3), open the needle valves re-pressure the tree then open the choke. It required everything to be done in the correct order to ensure the right pressure level. Everything depended on the preceding step and the availability of seals and other replacement equipment.

Get back on the boat and go to rig and visit a few minutes and go home beat and tired. When we got back to the dock, we finally found the replacement choke packing and found some at the plant, but they were not the kind needed. So, we called Houston and got chewed out. I called Point Noir, Gabon talked with a gentleman from Baker, and now, having been educated on choke packing, I called Houston and ordered the right equipment. When the packing showed up at the office, a fax was sent asking why I had not let Houston handle it. But since I was risking life and limb going up to change the packing, I was not in much humor, and the new packing showed up with the next person who came in from Houston. We could not wait in the actual conditions present in Malabo and had to be quick on our feet to get the job done without additional hassles.

The incident highlighted the challenges of remote operations. Frustration and miscommunication were part of the territory. However, it also underscored our determination to get the job done, even if it meant learning on the fly. We were always looking for robust solutions for small problems. There was never an easy way to do anything in the country. Yet, we always dealt with the issues one way or the other. My conversation with the Baker representative in Gabon was an impromptu lesson that ultimately saved the day.

In the end, the right choke packing arrived, but not without a few hiccups along the way. We ensured that the well was correctly packed, so there wouldn't be any trouble in the near future.

This experience taught us the importance of adaptability and resourcefulness in the face of unexpected obstacles. It was a reminder that in remote locations, problem-solving often required quick thinking and creativity, traits that defined our work in those challenging environments.

TANKER
KIAT

One of the next projects was to make a 4-point mooring system. The project required putting buoys in a pattern like a square and then pulling several million pounds against the anchor based on the length of the line, size, and weight of the anchor. The ship would start to pull on the anchor with so many tons for an amount of time, increasing the pull until it was determined to be sufficient for a 400,000 BBL tanker completely loaded, with an ocean current of a certain knot speed from a certain direction. However, it required strict control, and it was easy for things to go wrong at any given point in time.

The 10" pipeline had been broken when the ship was turned around and pulled one of the anchors across the pipeline, breaking it and causing the gas to come up under the ship, but the ship didn't lose its buoyancy and sink.

When the tanker entrance direction would be determined by the mooring master for the little tugboat to come in the port or starboard side or bow or stern to secure the tanker with the ropes first before the tug would come in and take the wire rope to the buoy determined by the mooring master to anchor the ship and prevent it from crashing into the shore, there was only one time when the current changed direction while the tanker was entering the mooring pattern. However, the mooring master and the tugboat captain being very experienced, knew where to run the lines to avert another catastrophe. Once the ship was in position, the loading lines were pulled up and attached to the ship, then the valves going to the stock tanks were opened to load the tanker at about 20,000 BPH (barrels per hour.) As the tanker was loaded, the ship sank into the ocean. After loading, the valves were closed, and the ship would be released and sail to the refinery, usually to Limba in Cameroon, but one time, it went to a refinery in the USA.

The ships ran small channels so that the petroleum products can be easily transported to processing facilities. The timing is important for goods like LPG. The right delivery at the right time ensures optimal value and gains for the involved companies.

PLATFORM

☙ • ❧

The getting on the platform landing without life preservers finally came to a conclusion when people from Houston came over and wanted to go to the platform until we got out there, and I bailed off the back of the tugboat and slightly mistimed my leap and banged my shoulder into the landing and finally climbed up on the land. The person from Houston wouldn't come on the landing, so we did the work needed and got back on the boat, where the question was asked why we didn't have life preservers, and the answer was no one would allow us to order them. When asked about not landing on the deck, we answered if we missed, we would either get back on the boat or climb onto the deck. But in no case did a person let go of the rope and fall into the water. So, there were no serious problems ever.

Later in 1995, there was one person who said he could do it, and he grabbed the blue rope and tried to swing on the landing. However, the rope dropped him into the ocean, and the barnacles on the landing chewed him up. But thankfully, he got lucky as the propeller on the tugboat narrowly missed him. The boat captain and I looked at one another. I said to the boat captain that I thought— he hadn't done that too many times and the captain said, "If ever!"

When we got to the platform production deck, he had meat hanging off his arms. So, he handed me his knife, and I cut the stringer off him. I guess he thought I was going to be sick to my stomach, but WAWA had taught me many hard lessons. So, an upset stomach from blood was not among them (I was on a flight from London to Paris when I was told Carrie

Fisher was on the flight, and when we got on the plane, I sat by her and her daughter. She was respectful and polite and had starred in a movie in Congo, so I told her about WAWA (West Africa Wins Again), and she told me about Congo that if it could, and it would go wrong. Well, these are things that I have always found true in Africa. You can face problems from the most unexpected situations. They can make you look silly and 'wanting' for answers you can never get.

MILITARY ENZIMA

The soldiers were always thinking of ways to try to get things, and it was never smart to tell them "No." But when you did, it had to be done with a kind tone of voice but stern showing, and not give in to them or be a coward and run off to your house and hide. This balance was pretty delicate, and we always had to find innovative ways to make them understand things. This was especially challenging when safety was concerned. Oil and gas exploration and delivery are fraught with dangers, and little carelessness can cause a massive incidence. So, here is a story about how we had to deal with the military personnel.

On one occasion, they were shooting squirrels out of the trees, but we explained the bullets might hit the oil tanks and blow up. So, we made another trip to the ministry, where it got settled that they would not be shooting at the squirrels, but we agreed to feed the soldiers. At the time, there were only three soldiers present there, so it seemed not much of a hassle. But the first thing we knew, we had about 15 as all the ones from the airport showed up and expected to be fed. Still, we took three meals down there and told them no more than three meals would be served. They got pissed, but we didn't budge, and after a few days, they quit showing up at lunch. And we were down to 1 or 2 soldiers, and the rest stayed away as that required traveling 2 to 4 miles for little or no food. Another time, they tried the same version of diesel for their truck – only this time, it was a different truck each day, as they would sell the diesel in town, so we gave them a marked

55-gallon drum, which they had to bring. But they tried that for a day or two, and then we made it, so they got 55 gallons. But the barrel was kept locked up with us, which became impractical, as it was too much work for them, so they stopped. So, this was how to deal with them on a consistent basis. You had to give ground and help them. But it was also important to hold onto the agreed terms and never give in to their exceeding demands all the time.

One time, they wanted to play chicken, so we met on the road, and I took my hand in before the mirrors hit the truck, but the other driver didn't, which was no longer a game they played. You can guess how it ended.

They also had a cumulative fish tax, which means if someone had a fish and the soldier didn't get it, he would try to get all the next person's fish. Our workers usually came on Friday or Saturday and asked me to take them home after fishing or catching red crabs. These workers were mostly kin to the President or had a brother who was high in the government. One night, one thought he had a political stroke, so he stopped us at Abayak, where they kept the tiger's teeth (steel spikes) across the roads. So, I invited him in, and we went to the jail, where we were greeted by a high official. We were released, but he was not. I don't know what happened to him, but he was not at Abayak the next night.

The workers would sell the fish in town or to our chef, but the crabs they would purge with corn and feed their families. My workers would fish off the platform as I made them lines with a steel leader and a hook to use. Most of the time, they caught barracuda, which would cut the rope, so the steel leader was needed. One time, they caught several in a few minutes. They would sell them to the boat crew as they were from the Orient and loved fish. We got to the port, offloaded our equipment into the truck along with the fish, and started up the hill to exit the port. The guards stopped us and tried to steal a fish, but I popped the clutch, and the truck lurched forward so that the guard got his fingers cut, but he got no fish. We could always get away with it because everyone knew the game. They could not press on, fearing that higher authorities may get involved. However, doing something harsh consistently meant taking undue chances as someone on the post could belong to the influential President's family, and this would mean dire results for us.

Another time, the captain bought him some beer, and they stopped us. And since the beer was in the floorboard and out of sight, the guards asked for a drink. But I didn't offer any, and as we drove away, the captain said he would have given them a bottle. To which I said, that was fine, but it wasn't my beer to give away, so I made no offer. So, these things kept happening. Since the local population generally strived for these facilities, turning to foreigners and multinational companies was often their go-to source to enjoy such luxuries.

On another occasion, a fishing boat we thought from Nigeria tied up to the buoys in the mooring area, causing the military ninjas to surround us around midnight, but they left before daylight. Then, the commander came out the next morning upset, accusing us of trying to steal oil. The boat was maybe 100 feet long by 20 feet wide by 10 feet deep, or 4,000 barrels total instead of the 400,000 barrels we normally loaded on the tanker. The commander started his speech but realized he was off base and left without his dash, but he got something out of the kitchen and left happy.

POLICE
POLISIA
(FANG)

⪜ • ⪝

The police were a bigger pain in the butt as we had a letter signed by President Obiang, saying, don't molest us unless we broke the law. They would hassle us, but if you played games with them, like when they asked for your vehicle papers, I would give them typing papers, newspapers, or toilet paper. And if I was really in a hurry, I would show them the presidential paper, and if they continued to be a pain, invite them into the truck and head toward the police station, and after one or two had been there, they would ask to get out or bail out when they got worried about going there. Therefore, we had to deal with using different methods on different occasions. Since resources were a minimum in the country, it was common for the police to try different things just to gain anything from foreigners or, generally, people who had something to give.

On the way back from the 21-day holiday being gone from Malabo, we took off from Paris to go to Douala. When we got off the plane, where everyone had French machine guns, so we headed down the airport to the passport and customs area when a soldier about 6'5" was walking in that direction to customs. A member of our group, about 3' tall, grabbed his hand and walked with him to the passport and customs area, but no one laughed or snickered at the sight of them walking through the airport to passport and customs. I stayed with the luggage to get it checked through the car to take us to the Sawa Hotel while others got in the car.

We wanted to go on a safari in Cameroon, so we went to a travel agent, and while sitting there, a man went into the bank to get money, and when he came out, two gentlemen tried to steal the money, but a bank security guard shot one in the leg. The police showed up, and one put his foot on the guy's leg and started pressing on it, so he ran out of blood. The guy asked the robber: what is your name, your friend's name, and where do you live before the guy died from the loss of blood. The police shot in the air to see if they could scare the guy's friend but to no avail. The police jumped in their car and drove off. The almost-robbed man dragged the dead guy out of the way, hopped in his car, and went home. Then the garbage truck pulled up, threw the guy in the truck, and went to the dump – saving the taxpayers for court and medical costs. Now, this was something interesting. Normal justice was carried out this way, typically in the country, and no one batted an eye.

One day, we came back from the platform, and I took both workers home. And the last lived in Younda or New Billy. I drove him to his place, and on the way in, there was a traffic police individual, so I let the last one out and proceeded back out to the road, where he stopped me. Since I was really tired from a day on the platform, I stopped and gave him my vehicle papers as well as the President's signed paper, but he held me up and wanted more, to which I decided he wasn't going to get. They were always looking to get something. We went at it for a few minutes, and then I looked up. Here came the last man's brother, who was the prime minister's personal bodyguard. So, he stood by for a few moments then he began talking Fang to the policeman. After he finished, the policeman said he was in traffic and not a presidential guard, so he shouldn't be bothered (this worried me because he had a loaded weapon, and the policeman didn't). If he shot the guy and the policeman had AIDS or Ebola, I could accidentally get it. Instead, he asked me if the policeman had seen my truck papers, and I answered, yes, sir. So, I gave them to him, and he slammed them into the policeman's chest.

And when the policeman stood there looking at the papers, the prime minister's guard grabbed the papers and shoved them in the window of the truck and said go. I left and was thankful. I went home and the next day went to the port for some boxes, but when I got to the first intersection near Hotel Urecha in town, there was the policeman with the right side of his head swollen, and when I drove by, he saluted me. It was several days before I got stopped again. So, this is how things were resolved in Equatorial Guinea. Every interaction was about the power game where everyone was looking to gain something. However, this all occurred due to the constant unavailability of resources to the common people of the country. The available things were stuck with only a few individuals, and only foreign companies working on projects had anything to spare for these hungry policemen.

Another time, Alba #2 had parted tubing, and we were going up to the platform. So, we loaded the equipment on the boat the night before, along with our workers, and were getting ready to leave when this drunken policeman walked up and started a fight with one of the workers from President Obiang's mainland home of Mongomo. Since he had a gun and none of us did, I shot us under the casing we had stacked on the dock and came out the other side while the wireline hand stood there with his mouth open. Our guy got his point across, and the fight ended so we could start on the platform. We made it and offloaded the equipment and made one run with the slick line and near dark, loaded up, and went to Abayak to call Houston, who wanted to have a conference call and since we had been run in the ditch by the presidential guards because the President landed after dark (the President would not land during daylight so that meant pre-dawn or after dark). We drove to Nautico – a restaurant at the old port. We made our order and waited, so the food arrived, and the phone call came in and was routed to us since the orders were given by someone that the call took precedence over all others (there were three international overseas lines). When I picked up the phone, the guy who had never been to

Equatorial Guinea, so he wanted to eat my ass out, and I was in no mood. So, since the slick line operator was a good friend of his, I asked the slick line operator to talk to him. He was kind and took the phone, but the big boss in Houston was not prepared for the discussion that followed. The big boss started off with why we were late leaving the dock, thinking I was going to get fed to the lions, but after the guy was told about the armed policeman attacking us and the fight that ensued, his attitude changed, and he knew it was not Kansas. So, the slick line guy also told him about getting run off the road. We left at daylight the following day and worked all day, returning after dark with no firm results. After the next day, we ran a metal clothes hanger in on the bottom of a wireline tool. It went in the clothes hanger alongside pointing up the side of the tool, and when it came out, the clothes hanger was hanging below the tool, meaning it had gone through a separated joint pipe. The minister called after I got back that night. The only thing he asked was if I could fix it, and I said, "No, sir." So, we were down to 3500 bopd and 47 mmcf of gas. There were things that we could fix, and then there were things that were not possible. With the problems you would face in Malabo, it wasn't always possible to carry out changes and stuff that would produce the best possible results.

Before the rig arrived, we had to do a bottom platform survey in case the last rig threw a pump liner overboard, which could punch a hole in the jack-up rig can. So, we loaded up the equipment and got to the platform, offloaded the equipment, and discovered they were missing some of the equipment, which I told them we would get it tomorrow. They said tonight, but this wasn't the USA, and they knew better. So, when we got back to the dock, we found the armed guard, and they thought they were going to demand the equipment, to which they found was not going to happen as the guard explained in Fang that it was not happening. So, the next day, I got the missing equipment out of the warehouse and on the boat. The surveyors went to the beach and drank some and got some sun. We left with no trouble, got to the platform, offloaded the equipment, and began to survey the ocean floor around the platform. One of the gentlemen was young and had gotten too much sun, so when one of my men was laughing and joking and hit the guy on the shoulder, he dropped to the deck, and my guy became worried, but I looked at him and said no problem and grabbed my dictionary to look up the Spanish for sunburn (bronceado) and something my guys had an idea about. We got through with that bottom survey part, got all the equipment offloaded, and headed back to town.

The company brought in a rig and fixed the problem, and a new operator was selected since the government wanted the LPG portion of the project to be started. So, it all depended on the needs of the project and the direction that the President was willing to take. If the government truly desired something, it would quickly facilitate companies and people and allow them to start something new in a record time, especially for the conditions of Equatorial Guinea.

Therefore, the LPG project brought in lots of new people with no experience in Africa, but they got a short course in West African construction and economics. Things were never straightforward in the region. You could face problems that were simply not present in other parts of the world. I will go on to say that sometimes, these kinds of problems were not even present in other parts of Africa or even some terrible places in East Asia like North Korea.

Planning for people to stay, eat, sleep, bathe, and get medical treatment was a monumental task. Since there was no grocery store and the meat came from France, Douala, Gabon, or Nigeria. Everything was planned since most of the people were from the USA, and everything being at a finger snap away, understanding was not part of their common sense. The shots or vaccines were supposed to be obtained as our supply was limited, and like tetanus was limited, they could be dead in a few hours if infected with tetanus. Hepatitis A & B vaccines were not readily available, but some showed up with Hepatitis B immunity, which meant they had not had the vaccine but caught the disease from a wildlife style. These are diseases that hit pretty hard when someone gets it for the very first time. If not immune, these diseases can result in the death of the person. There are so many things that can go wrong in such instances. The best way is to stay away from the local population or ensure that you have immunity against all the major viral diseases.

One of our cooks got released by the doctor because of that, and people were not happy since, or anything made with eggs, they could not have eggs sunnyside up or not cooked hard or pies or cakes or bread. The bread on the island was made from Canadian flour, which was softer than flour from Russian flour, which Africa got since the Russians got it for hard currency like butter they got from Europe, then reprocessed it into a poorer quality and better quality from which Africa got crap. We would get "Biddle" brand butter from France, which was good and readily available. We didn't get sirloin or ribeye since it was not available after the South African ranchers left. They had their cattle heard on the mountain above Luba. We drove up there, and since there were no mosquitoes because it was cool, and we met them and sat on their couch while the clouds floated through their living room. Sometimes, we would lose sight of them as the clouds were thick.

The trip from Malabo to the top of the mountain was something as the road was not wide enough for two vehicles, and when you were on the right side of the road, if you got off the road, your vehicle would go into the ocean, and the left side would send you into the mountain. We were going to Luba, which was in the southern part of the island. We came around a curve to see a Land Rover with a young man standing on the back bumper with half of his body in my lane. My choices were to drive over the cliff, drive into the mountain, drive into the Land Rover, or hit the young man. He pivoted as I got within inches, so instead of hitting him, I passed within inches of him but didn't hit him. We continued on down to Luba to see the city and the beach.

We saw the beach, which was beautiful, and the stream from the caldera flowing through the city, and we noticed the sea turtles (Kulu or ku – Fang for turtle), they had them stacked in the stream with a piece of rope around the flipper and if they were left too long, the flipper would rot off, and they would tie the rope on another flipper until they would be eaten. We went by the white sand beach or Arina Blanca, where Fernando Poo first landed when he discovered the island. The area had a lot of history, but for us, it was all about the sea turtles.

We left Luba and drove up to Malabo, where the South Africans had the cattle ranch. On the way up, we saw a lady, and since we didn't have other than a verbal map, we stopped and asked her where Malabo was in my broken Spanish, but she answered in the king's English accent and all talked about shocked. But we got up to the ranch, visited with the man and his wife, then headed down the mountain toward Malabo and the camp.

CONSTRUCTION

The people who showed up to build the LPG plant were used to building it, but not in Africa. Now, this was a major hurdle. Working in West Africa had its unique challenges. It was difficult to procure equipment and materials on a short deadline, and everything had to be already available when starting a new task, especially when building an LPG plan. When we started talking about the cost, they mentioned a cost number, and I asked them if that was a USA-based cost. They didn't argue, so I explained what I had seen, and they understood. It was explained to me that the cost was best for AFE (Authorization For Expenditure). If you ran the cost numbers based on USA cost and then tripled it ($1 times 3). As a result, they thought I was nuts and used 30%, which blew up to 100% one-third of the way through the project. It is so difficult to make people believe that it was how things worked in Malabo. Each task faced bureaucratic delays in the country. You needed to find the right Presidential channel to get things done. You needed quick support from your company if you wanted some stuff. However, it is true that there were profits involved, so American companies would keep working in Equatorial Guinea for these great sums.

We also faced many equipment problems during our project. A perfect example was when we went to build the stand for the diesel pump. It was designed out of the Halliburton red book, which was great for cementing casing in the ground but not making a diesel pump stand – why? Because the cement was not designed for foundation building but for oil industry casing. So, the form was built, and the cement prepared, then poured in the form and was allowed to harden according to the chart. As the wooden boards were taken off, the form started to fall on the ground. There were multiple problems with it. One, the cement was not oilfield certified, and two, the black sand was from the beach, which had salt in it from the ocean. It was not certain what percent of salt was in there, and since the salt percent is not known, the pump foundation fell apart.

This was not all lost as the very large foundations that were needed for the large LPG towers saved all this from being a disaster. But WAWA was not through but was only getting started as the cement was now being mixed by the local cement trucks. So, the lessons continued. Wow, I never thought I could learn so much from a single project. They ordered a volume of cement, and when the trucks showed up, they started pouring from the trucks, and several things became evident – one, the cement was not the USA quality, the truck volume was incorrect, and the boulders in the cement needed crushing. The quality was solved by ordering different cement, but the truck volume was a different matter on two matters. One, the inside of the truck was cemented up, reducing the volume, but that led to another problem. The decision was made to chip the inside of the truck drum out, as there were several areas where the chipping became excessive.

In a few days, the inside was cleaned, and the cement chipped out. So that was when WAWA showed up. They wanted to wash out the drum, and that is when WAWA showed its ugly head. Where they had been, the cement that was chipped out there looked like a showerhead. As the drum turned, the water came out looking like a spray. But fortunately, being construction professionals, they had run into this before but not on this scale, so they knew what to do. After solving the problem, they needed crushed rocks, which they got a rock crusher that was found in the area and brought to us. The rocks were another story as there was no source for rocks as the island was volcanic, and picon or cinder rock was plenty but not for foundation cement. The children down the road in the village were complaining about getting pencils and paper. The chief came and said the children wanted this, but he thought they should have to work for it. So then, how were the rocks supposed to be collected, and the children paid for their volume, not getting paid for the work of other kids? We thought and came up with a pile of rocks as we measured height and base, so basically, it was measuring a cone. Where did they get the rocks but off our road? Each child would stand by their pile as they gave the collector their name, and the pile was measured and recorded. If the child was younger, we would add an extra inch or two to even things out. This worked out well.

Now that we had a cement truck and crushed rocks, the forms were constructed, and the rebar was installed. Since we didn't have a rebar bender, a welder's blowtorch was used to bend the 1" or larger rebar, and then it was wired in place. Then, on the day of the pour, they asked for a bucket to measure the water needed to not over-dilute the cement. So, they were given a bucket, which proved to work. Still, the problem was it was too slow since cement will set up once the water and cement mix, so the bucket was dropped, and the water hose was turned to full stream as the operation needed to be shortened as it was a big pour and repeating it was not in the schedule. So, as the operation was going to be lengthy from start to finish, we brought caramel popcorn as none of us had seen anything like this, and there was nothing else going on, and not many had a TV. We sat, watched the operation, and had caramel popcorn. We finally got everything to work, and the first tower foundation form was poured, and now all there was to wait for the cement to harden. The remaining forms went off without WAWA again.

Another incident caused very serious injury for one of our workers when he tried to cut the top of a 55-gallon methanol drum with a blowtorch. He was over the drum and started cutting on the side with the small hole, which meant he was standing over the large hole when the methanol fumes caught fire, and the drum was enlarged, and he got first-degree burns. They brought him down to the camp where I was, and we got into the car, but as we started to drive away, he said something, and I asked what, to which it was explained he needed to get his chicken wings (another story yet to be explained). He and the wings got in the vehicle, and down the road we went, wings, first-degree burns, and all, to the Doctor's office. We got to the airport, and I saw a lady missionary nurse from Brownsville, TX. So, she gets in, and off we go. I have never been around someone with first-degree burns. So, we are driving along as quickly and safely as possible, and he is hanging out the window with his skin blowing off. Finally, the lady said to quit being a baby to the guy who was hanging out the window to cool off from the burns, with his skin blowing off. So, I said the same thing; as we drove to the clinic, I let them out and went and parked. I went back inside to check on the burned person, and I saw they were smearing brownish cream on him, and I thought maybe he was going to be eaten. So, I got scared and left.

The chicken wings were bad juju to the natives as they thought if they ate them, their children would be deformed. So, we told them no different but ordered wing sauce, and life was good until someone ate one. Then the genie was out of the bottle, and it wasn't going back in. Now, no one would stop eating them. All the local customs usually get lost when things are tasty. We enjoyed the situation and tried to play around it. We tried to tell them they might have deformed children, which they said they had enough children, or the woman was barren, so we went from excess wings to plenty cause the French nor the Cameroonians or Nigerians knew about the wing myth. The worker was terminated since he violated safety rules, but he was paid termination pay (his son helps with the fang words that are used in this book.

BINGA OBEEBEE WOMEN FARMING

The farming along the road was done mostly by women cause of the social order in the tribes and villages. They came up and asked if we would make them a farm, and since we were not farmers, we blew that off. And, like the rock program, the village chief finally came up. It explained that they needed us to take our D-9 Cat and push back the brush two blades wide. That way, they could go in with machetes and clean the ground and plant the malanga, yucca, banana, and plantain, and a green plant that looked like green greens for salad. The women were very hardy since they slept on the farms with the boas, cobras, and mambas. They could take on quite challenging tasks. In fact, they could take on any task and complete it. They were used to carrying out physical tasks that required considerable effort.

What was funny was that the Peace Corps was supposed to come over and help with farming, road building, and medical assistance, but they didn't have a farmer, civil engineer, or medical person in the bunch. There was no way they were actually equipped to carry out any good in the community. They did not even offer a temporary solution. They would go out to the villages, stay a short time, come in for a party at Nautico, stay in town, then go back to the jungle. The few times I would approach them to talk with them. They called us bad names as we were raping the land and the people, but all I saw was they came in, tried to fit in with the locals, then got corn rows, and seemed to get pregnant and go home.

The ladies we would offer to take them to town since they were carrying 70 lbs. in their wicker baskets, plus their children. The children were bow-legged since the kids were around the mother's waist about 7 miles from town to the farm. We would ask the mothers to meet us by the river since the lazy men were at the airport and would not help the women (some did, but very few). I would help load the wicker basket into the truck. That is how I knew the weight of the basket. One of the ladies had a little boy she named Little Mike, but he died of malaria or one of the many diseases. The planting started in January after the dry season in mid-October or November through mid-January or February.

We would look up and see the smoke coming out of the jungle, and within 2 to 3 weeks, the rains would start, and the next growing season was on. The ladies would be muddy from all their work, but they would ride with me by removing their muddy clothes and washing them in the river or having another set of clothes. I would wear overalls or coveralls with a slit up the side, and every once in a while, one of them or a child would stick a finger or hand in the slit to see if I was white, and yes, it did startle me because they had their doubts and it shocked them as well. One missionary was outside taking a shower, and the kids got in the tree to see if they were white all over. This was the type of stuff that would occur from time to time. There were always those who took advantage of the local community and their struggles. It was common for people to get intrigued when seeing white people, so they would love to find out more about them.

MALARIA

Malaria is very common in Africa. I had malaria six times – five while in Africa and once in the USA after spending 35 days in Africa. Palasidium vivax, malariae, ovale, and knowlesi are the most common, but it is most curable or preventable with quinine and curable with halfane (French drug), and preventable with mefloquine (USA). Doxycycline is 98% preventable when used daily against malaria. Palisidium falciparium is resistant to chloroquine because the natives don't complete the treatment but take it in a partial treatment. The malaria season in Bioko was mid-February or March to mid-October to mid-November basically during the dry season. The most common prevention was long-sleeved shirts and pants, as, during World War II, the Germans suffered 30% to 40% less malaria than the French and British due to using longer shirts and pants. Also, the natives believed they could build resistance to malaria, which is untrue. Falciparium, I had once and was given artesunate – a Chinese herb which got rid of it in me but required one capsule treatment for a week and an injection of artesunate (looks like ground-up green grass), one week of Haldane pills. I was given ground-up fruit drink several times a day to help my liver, kidneys, dehydration, and bowels. My temperature got to 102 degrees, but it fell back from there. There were several people in Malabo who were greatly harmed by brain damage – one man and one lady. I don't know the man, but stories varied, as he was harmed by the police or malaria, and he looked like or acted like it was high temperature from malaria, instead of police injury, but the local Macians used this against President

Obiang. The man wore a plastic Kaiser pointed helmet with one mid-calf boot and a roadside tennis shoe. One of our expats was startled by the man when our expat went out, got drunk, and fell asleep in a lawn-type chair on the roadside. He never went back out and did that I knew of. The lady I was told was a former school teacher whose temperature from malaria got too high, which was what caused her to have brain damage.

We had a worker who was and had a good sense of humor. He admired Michael Jackson, would wear his hair like Michael, and wore glasses. But he had no lenses, and all the new arrivals would look at him and wonder if their eyesight was failing them until they asked another expat, which would bring a roar of laughter as the question was usually asked about at chow in the mess hall. Somebody made up a comment about Michael, and so he decided to quit making Michael his ideal.

He liked to play jokes on us expats, but the natives said he had a girlfriend, which I don't know if it was true. However, he started the rumor, I had a girlfriend, and I asked him what her name was and who she was. Well, he finally told me her name was Gloria and told me where she lived. So, I started looking for her, and finally, one day, I spotted the lady who I was told was a former school teacher who had contracted malaria and was hurt by high temperature. So, I told him I found Gloria, and he was shocked. Gloria would clean car mirrors and metal lamp posts and go back and forth from the airport with a blanket being laid on the highway. Of course, when new expats came in, they would ask why she was doing this. We told them she worked for the CIA, and it was a secret code to the satellites for on-island secrets.

One disease, filariasis is particularly terrible. We had one case I knew of during my four years there. It was on the side of one of our worker's faces. It is known as elephantiasis, as the worms grow and make certain areas of the body swell hugely. The Europeans would put people in the hospital with blood drained out of one arm, then filter it, treat the blood to kill or remove the worms, and put it back in the other arm. I heard it was a long process.

The Spanish had a series of medicines they would use to treat the patients, and it would cause the worms to come out of the patient. In this case, since it was on the side of the head, the worms would come out of the ears, eyes, nose, and mouth, where the patient would look like a sort of Medusa.

We had CNN news with Debra Marchini but no satellite movies, so we finally got a Bluetooth disc player. One of the first movies was "The Addams Family." The movie started—everyone gathered around until the "hand" came down the hall, and everybody disappeared. All we heard was "white man juju," and when the hand would reappear, everyone would disappear again.

Another event was when the automatic bread maker showed up. They were set on the frontmost table, and the ingredients were placed in the machines and turned on. The machine would stir the ingredients and then slowly heat up the ingredients, and the bread would begin to bake. The people would stand mesmerized by the machine as they had never heard or seen anything like that.

Many dangerous incidents kept occurring on the oil exploration platform. Many of them were routine events, while some were more dangerous than others. However, two events on the platform almost cost me my life.

The first event happened when the flowline blew off the header. We came to the platform, which was enveloped in fog-like conditions, coming from one of the block valves that had washed out due to flow corrosion caused by the velocity of the gas, condensate, and water flowing out of the formation into the 4 1/2" tubing thru the tree into the flowlines into the block valves then into the 10" pipeline where the glycol solution pumped from the plan would be injected into the 10" pipeline. It kept the flowline from freezing while the mixture was transported to the separation facilities at Punt Europa. I got on the landing deck, climbed the ladder to the platform, and shut the wells in. The other workers came up and were watching, ready to help me when required. With the wells shut in, I got ready to start rigging down the block valves. So, I shut the one in that was spewing vapor into the air. This was when the problem started, as with the block valve closed, the flowline started to pressure up since the trees had not cooled off enough for the valves to seat. It shut off all flow completely from the downhole. I called out to my helper, asking in Spanish, "Valvula es Cerra" (valve is closed in Spanish). Before I could open the needle valves, the pressure built up so rapidly that the whistling sound started, and there was a "pop", which was the flowline blowing off in front of me, throwing me 1-2 feet back against the back of the header. I was unconscious. When I came to it, it was kind of like the way Tom Hanks was depicted in "Saving Private Ryan" when the mortar or bomb knocked him out on D-Day – at the end of the movie, after he was knocked unconscious again. Before I came back to consciousness, I heard "not yet," and after coming to my senses, I woke up to the hot gas, water, and condensate blowing in my face. When I got up, I was cussing like a sailor in a bar. Everybody started paying attention and quickly secured all the problems to eliminate the danger present. One of my workers standing in front of the flowline had his coveralls cut; it looked like a razor blade had made the cut every ¼" from his thigh to his ankle. After everything was secure, I realized my right glass lens was missing along with my cloth hat, and I looked like I had been shot with no. 9 bird shot from my left hip across my chest to my right shoulder. We started getting people on the boat and headed back to town. When we got back to the port, we met the doctor. One of the workers couldn't walk, but the doctor told him to get up, and he did (kind of like that guy Jesus told a sick man to get up and walk, and he did, too). Then we went to the doctor's office. There were several people in the room when we came in, and they looked at us and were whispering after looking at me with my wounds about the government shooting the white people. The good doctor got us cleaned and patched up. The next day, we went back to the platform and started tearing down the damaged equipment while new flowlines were built.

Another time, a night storm came through and broke one of the flowlines off where it was attached at the choke on the tree. We got out there, and the noise level was nothing I had ever heard. We didn't have gas masks. So, I wrapped a red handkerchief around my head. It seemed to work, so we got in the boat and started paddling to the platform, hoping to climb up on the landing deck. Then I got to the deck, climbed on the tree, and shut them in. We started off with my two helpers, a wireline hand, a Ghanaian, a Cameroonian, and myself, but the flow made about a 4' to 6' hole in the ocean, which blew us to the left side of the landing deck and I missed hooking the landing deck by about 2' to 4'. So, we went past the platform and paddled back to the tug boat. We got back on the boat and, recovered from the nervous ordeal and got a better plan. We regained our courage, moved further to the right of the landing deck, and began our second attempt. Everything was going as planned, and then I noticed we were off course, heading too near the hole in the ocean, so I looked up to get my directions and noticed we were to the far right of the landing deck. Therefore, I turned to notice the Ghanaian's paddle had broken, and the Cameroonian was paddling us right into the hole in the ocean. So, I got his attention to quit paddling, and I got my 20' pole and began digging us out of the hole and around the platform. As I had looked up to get our position, the handkerchief had blown up, and I got a big gulp of produced fluids in my mouth and down my lungs, but I hung in there, and we made it back to the boat. We all got back on the boat and started discussing plan #3. We were already shaken but not at all looking to accept failure. I asked for a drink of water and drank heartily, but it caused me to throw up. I got drunk and fell down. At this point, it was decided to return to the dock. After arriving at the dock, I was taken to the staff house, where the US embassy had provided us with oxygen. My skin turned green and blue from the fluids building up in my body. I lay on the bed with a Ringer's lactate drip in one arm, glucose in the other, and oxygen flowing through the nasal cannula. My head rested flat against the bed with my arms and legs elevated. I had two African doctors standing talking in Spanish, saying, "zapatos y manos es azul and verde" (his feet and hands are blue and green). The produced oil could be slowly gotten out of my system. The next day, I was better, and the new flowlines were being installed. My lungs were burnt from the produced fluids, and my breathing capacity was low. The new lines were installed but were destroyed in less than 12 hours, and the platform was shut in by the ESD (emergency shut-down), which is a valve on the wing of the tree which is closed when the hydraulic fluid that holds it open is cut off. This was one of the last times I was involved with the platform, as the new management was taking over, and my time was not needed.

On another occasion, I was at the old port when the children came running down the hill leading from the President's palace with the chimp running behind them. At first, I thought, but as the chimp came by, a child broke his arm running from the chimp. Actually, the chimp ran by after the child got between my legs, which was dumb of me because the chimp would have killed me. And the chimp was just trying to run down the hill. The child stayed with me for a few minutes, and then, with his arm swaying, he went up the hill. After a while, the presidential guards came and got the chimp by the chain, took it up to the palace, and put the chimp in his place. I thought this was for show, but I heard the chimp was an alarm of sorts, as it would throw rocks at people if they got near or raise a ruckus if someone came into the area.

During Christmas, they would take champagne to the President, and then I was told to roll up my window, but not why. I would settle down without knowing the reason, and I soon got the reason when a monkey threw a rock at the car, hitting the top of the door frame and not breaking the glass or hitting me.

The camp ladies went to town, and on the way, the local ladies were selling ground beef on the side of the road. The locals called it ground beef because it lived in the ground and tasted like beef when fried with garlic. The ground beef was 12" to 18" long plus tail.

One Sunday, a large crowd gathered for the arrival of the Iberia flight from Madrid around noon to 1 p.m. Normally, it was non-eventful, but on one Sunday, I guess due to all the people being in tall grass in front of the airport, the ground beef ran into the crowd of people waiting for the Iberia airplane to land. The ground beef would run into the crowd and hit us in the shoes or boots, and work it was back, almost to the cover, and stop. The plane landed, people deplaned, and then the attention shifted to the ground beef when it was urgent to capture it for the next meal. There was a mad rush for the animal, but it was finally caught.

Before the people got on or off the plane, they would go to the duty-free stands. The stands had cigarettes for sale one at a time and a shot of beer, soft drink, or other drinks available, but I never saw any of it cold.

Marriage for the natives was typical when they married in the church as the men took a wife, and that was the only one he got married in the church with, but the native marriages were different.

The man would decide he loved or wanted to marry a woman, and the courtship was on. And then, if he wanted to marry her, he went to the father and negotiated with him for a price that he would or may have already negotiated with her for the amount of money he would provide for her to rent a place or apartment with her providing food and taking care of the children. Now, if he didn't provide the agreed-upon amount, the police would usually come on Friday and beat the husband with a whip or branch, which would leave cuts on the husband's back. There was one man I could always tell had more than one wife because he was constantly exhausted. I would explain to him that a man with one wife would not be so tired. But since he had more than one wife, he never got rest as one was gripping in his face and two he had one in the face and one in one ear, then three wives he had one in his face and one in each ear. He would turn up missing on Friday but come to work on Saturday with cuts on his body. On Friday, I would make sure there was sulfur sauve and antibiotics to treat his wounds. I would recommend he get rid of one or two, but the strange thing was the men kept all the children. If the man took the wife back, he got his money back from the father.

One of our workers lived with one woman for a while to make sure she could treat the child well, as his wife had died, and he wanted to ensure she knew what to do.

One of the workers lived with a married couple, and he slept with the woman at night while the man worked, and the man slept with the woman during the day; the St. Elizabeth's Catholic

Cathedral Church in Malabo is beautiful. The gentleman who painted it was very gifted, considering he was not a trained artist. The church is named after St. Elizabeth of Hungary. It was started in 1378 and completed in 1508.

There were many paintings in the cathedral ceiling.

There were riots only two times, I remember, in Malabo, and none had anything to do with the government. Both times, it had to do with the currency Cafa or Central African Franc. Once, the CFA went from 100 to 200 CFA against the dollar, and everything in the country that came from outside got incredibly expensive. The bread was the biggest problem as its prices shot up and doubled in price, but the problem was solved when the bread size was cut in half, and the price for a bus ride stayed the same. Since the bread made from Canadian wheat was of high quality instead of Russian wheat, which would leave your gums hurting and bleeding (you could use it to almost drive nails).

The other was when the guy on the mountain forgot to collect what was in the mountain tank and forgot to open the valve to the city. Another problem was the tank would run dry, but it was usually because of valve operation. We were asked to help, but that was a trap. The people would go crazy once something was given to them, so we didn't want the responsibility. Also, the people in the jungle would hack into the lines when they got drunk on kiki (a palm sap that was high in sugar and made into liquor easily). The jungle version was clear, but once it got into town, it turned brown and could be deadly. If placed in the freezer, the jungle version would be a slush and not freeze. The trees would do this twice a year.

RIOTS
CURRENCY

❧ • ❧

One time, an expat was griping for cream in his coffee. And after a few days of listening to the guy bitch about it, a solution was found. But when the guy found it was breast milk, he blew up and spit it out and didn't bitch anymore.

Dairy products were something we all missed. One example was ice cream—there was no milk from cows on the island. Therefore, we had no way of making any ice cream. I never knew that having ice cream could be a luxury, but that was what I learned working in West Africa.

Once, while staying at the Sawa Sawa Hotel on our way back to Malabo through Douala, we watched a monkey at breakfast, slyly plotting to steal from a man engrossed in his paper.

Then, the fellow was on the other side of a small wall from the monkey, which the monkey would hide behind, look over the top, and then duck down. This went on several times, and then the monkey jumped over the wall, grabbed the rolls, and was off to the races.

LOCAL PRODUCE

Malabo has a wide variety of agricultural products. Before oil was discovered, these were the most common products available in Equatorial Guinea. It is common to find many fruits, vegetables, and other agricultural goods on the island where Malabo is located.

Malanga is commonly eaten in the entire region. It is a tuberous root that people typically plant in the region and eat in place of potatoes. Although they may not be as tasty or well-known as potatoes, they are a staple diet of the region. Yuca is another woody shrub, which is cultivated in this region. It is commonly eaten in the entire West African region, including all parts of Equatorial Guinea.

We all know about bananas and plantains. These are the starchy foods that are planted and eaten almost around the entire world. Banana typically refers to the type that we consume directly or after letting it ripen. On the other hand, plantains are harvested and eaten in the cooked form. They are a common variety to be eaten with all types of food groups. It is a common delicacy to have with fish and other meats, while the fried form is also quite popular in Equatorial Guinea.

Although mango is a more common fruit in Asia, African mango is abundantly found in this region. Typically, it is slightly different from the more famous Asian varieties, but it is a local delight to have in the summertime. Another great fruit is pineapple which grows quite well in rich volcanic soils, similar to the one found outside Malabo. It can be eaten right after plucking and is a great luxury to have under all circumstances.

Now, if we discuss the other fruits in the region, the common names that come to mind include papaya and avocado. These plants hold more medicinal value. We grew papaya trees on our compound as they offered excellent value for malaria patients. We would give such patients papaya or its juice, which helped speed up their recovery from viral infections. Avocado is also a great fruit with excellent food value. Our chef made guacamole from it, which tasted great. Although he would always call his dish Guatemala, which I told him was a country and not the name of a dish! But he would always believe that it was called that. Well, the point is, we could have it from time to time, but on a more usual basis like our own papayas.

Some other plants that were of more value included breadfruit and sawa sawa, Breadfruit is a variety of jack fruit, commonly found in many parts of the world. It is often used to make curries or to add flavor to other recipes. It is named so because it tastes like freshly baked bread with its starchy flavor. On the other hand, sawa sawa fruit is the one I didn't like much. It looks like an overgrown strawberry and tastes somewhere between a berry and a pineapple. Many people love it but I was not among them.

Cocoa is the chocolate bean plant famous all over the world. Strangely, the locals didn't use much of this plant. I was surprised to find that the area had some of the richest cocoa in Africa. The beans were dried on a special shale plate and tasted absolutely amazing. I would go on to say that the processed cocoa from the Sampaca Plantation tasted like Hershey's. The island also had so many coffee trees. They were so fragrant and super strong. However, their flowers only blossomed for a day.

CEO
CHEWING ME OUT

಄ • ೞ

I was in the Ministry of Mines and Hydrocarbons, and this CEO from another company came down the hall. So, I stopped and introduced myself to offer my help with his upcoming drilling program, but he used bad language. He kept telling me I was raping the country, so I excused myself and left him. He later got malaria and almost died while his employee had his vehicle broken into while enjoying the company of the owner of the Gamba de Orea. We used to go to the Gamba de Orea because the owner would keep the hookers run off from troubling us. After Mobil got there, the hookers demonstrated the Malabo handshake, which was simple. They would grab your genitals and move up and down like they were shaking hands. They tried this with me, and their answer was yes. But since I had seniority, I said no. In addition, they knew about the connections with the police, so I just said no, and they backed off. I suppose it was a good problem to have for people who did not care for their bodies and ready to enjoy all the pleasures of working in such a country.

The President's brother was a nice man to deal with, as I was asked to do small things for him, like get him a plastic drum for his water supply on the roof. But from time to time, we faced much more serious issues than some water storage solutions. It was when they arrested our worker and stole his red wing boots because he was supposed to have said something, and he was dragged from work when he was needed and held in jail minus his boots. We took him food to show our support for him, as there was nothing you could say or do as he had killed his uncle, cut him up in 6 pieces, and buried him in different spots so he didn't come back to life, then shot the cabinet ministers before turning to his brother and saying you are President – who would argue with him? He was head of police, military personnel, and court system. He had the reputation of running a good investigation and a fair court to reach a verdict. We had a soldier who was found guilty of stealing boots from our camp, and they caned him. They bent him over a soldier's guard station wall and beat him on his legs with a bamboo pole about 5' long and 2" in diameter until the bamboo was in shreds. Blood was running down his legs, and he could not walk but crawled down the road. We didn't have another event like that occur while I was there. We later found out it was the village chief's daughter who was the thief. But since she was the chief's daughter, she could not or was not beaten for the crime.

The other person we stayed away from was known to carry out punishment as he beat them until they broke down and then had their head busted like watermelons.

One of the President's bodyguards was a huge fellow who could have played offensive or defensive linemen in the NFL. He would come out and be on guard while the President would fly in or out of the airport. We found out one morning, he had gotten high on drugs and killed a friend of 20 plus years and had brain, heart, and liver cut before taking him to the hospital and dumping him at the hospital where when the doctor ran out, the man said, "He is dead." And the doctor said, seeing the man in front of him cut open and his skull flopping, "Yeah, he is dead!" The man would come to our camp to eat breakfast, lunch, or dinner and stand in line to be served and to realize I was close to being a meal.

On another occasion, the US ambassador got on national radio at night and said we should overthrow the government on national radio. I got up the next morning to go to the docks to retrieve some cargo, and when I got near Hotel Urecha, I was surrounded by 15 soldiers armed with AK-47s. In Spanish, they explained to me that I was a bad man, and I was thinking, what have I done now? I didn't know what I did, but I sure as hell wasn't going to do it again tonight. They eventually let me go, and when I got back to the camp, one of our employees whose brother had a high job in the government told me about the reason for the trouble. After that, I didn't cooperate with the US ambassador. One time, he asked me if I knew how much money we gave the President. I truthfully responded that I didn't know because it wasn't my duty to see checks or make any payments. Another time, he asked if I knew what percentage we paid the President per our contract, to which I told him no, I didn't, as I had not seen the contract as it wasn't my responsibility. Sure, I had been told some number, but I didn't know what the contract said. Even if I knew, it wasn't my place to tell them these numbers as they were only interested in their political games and not some steps that would actually improve the local community.

We had a worker who wanted to be an employee, and he was very happy when the day arrived. But when he got his first paycheck, he was upset and asked to speak to me. Through an interpreter, he asked why I was stealing his money and asked if I could see his paycheck since I had signed it. There it was present: the government deduction! So, I explained to him that he was now a registered taxpayer in the country and helped pay for his brother's salary. He was neither thrilled nor happy!

LOCAL ANIMALS

There were many issues with the local animals as well as they could make the working conditions impossible. For example, I was shocked to hear that snakes would commonly swallow rats, as there were plenty of them in our facilities. Instead, I asked Houston, our head office, to send mothballs – the solution everyone uses to get rid of dead rats in a civilized manner. This would allow us to stay away from using cobras and boas on our property roofs and always face the worry of getting bitten in some desolate land with no access to a credible medical solution. So, we got on a conference call, told them the situation of facing dead rats, and quickly got the required mothballs. However, the people at Houston were quite intrigued and wanted to know if it really was necessary to send so much of this product. But when we shared the absurd situation and how much stress it was causing in the office, we were relieved when the next person who came from Houston to Malabo came with a fresh supply of mothballs for us.

They also had boa constrictors on the island. The 20' boas long were not as big of a problem since they ate larger animals, but there were fewer of them. Moreover, they never seemed to be around our operations. They mostly remained near dense vegetation and didn't like areas that were too near the coast. They seemed to be mostly around the airport and were chopped up when the natives found them anywhere. These natives also had a good method to capture them in the jungle. I was really surprised with it and would love to use it myself sometimes. I plan on trying to get a patent on it, as I think it would work well here in the USA.

Green mambas were bad to deal with as they were pretty small – 2 to 3 feet long. They could ambush anyone as they were quite difficult to spot, especially in the trees. They would often stay in the coconut trees, waiting for the weaver birds to come into range. They were very hard to notice since they were green, mixed in with green vegetation. They wore the perfect camouflage.

Weaver birds were cute little birds like the Baltimore Robin. They make fancy nests that have to be woven intricately to attract a female, impress her to mate with the male, and lay eggs in the nest. But they could be a nuisance as they would keep chirping and make everyone's life difficult. But we didn't have BB guns to shoot them, so we got some small stones and pelted them so they would leave.

The crows or tuxedo birds were not anything more than just an island oddity. They looked like the American crow, but think of one who is dressed up in a tuxedo.

The native funerals were an experience since they borrowed our trucks. They didn't have cars to carry the dead and take them to the burial grounds. If the person died in the morning, they were usually buried in the afternoon or evening. The casket would be rented, loaded in the vehicle, and all the mirrors covered with cloth, so the dead could not see where they were going. There was not any pre-burial preparation in their culture. One Spanish man died and was literally put on ice until arrangements could be made to get him back to Spain.

Lizards were everywhere and were multicolored. Of course, they would eat the bugs and other items found in the forest. They were not a trouble for us, as they were just colorful creatures to look at.

Dikdik antelope were small, about 6" to 9" tall and maybe 12" long. They were hard to see or find since they could hide very easily in the foliage of the plants. Many people would catch them for home meals and sell them in the market. While at a cocoa plantation, I saw one that had been roasted on an open fire. The lady took it out, peeled the skin off like a paper wrapper, and ate it like a chicken leg. Through her hospitality, she offered me some, but I refused.

Malanga and yuca are root tubers that are commonly eaten in many parts of the world, including South America, Asia, and Western Africa. They are root tubers like potatoes that were grown just like them in the rich volcanic island soil. The people used them in everything they ate and cooked to eat. I never personally ate any food made from it, but I helped load the baskets of the ladies working on farms, which weighed about 70 lbs.

Their green salads looked like spinach but had no taste like it, nor did it taste like it nor like lettuce. It looked like poke salad that grew in cow lots in eastern Texas. I remember seeing poke salad when I was a kid, but I don't remember eating it in a salad. I remember that they were typically steamed like collards or mustard greens. They were cooked twice with the water poured out to remove the bitter taste. It made their taste more palatable, although I never liked them altogether, especially at a young age.

Bananas and plantains were a common staple of the native diet. The plants were easy to grow, and harvesting them was simple. Fresh bananas were fabulous. The plantain could be cut, sliced, and fried to make very good-tasting potato chips. These plants are revered by populations around the world for their nutritional value and easy accessibility. You will commonly find them in places like South Asia and East Asia, where they are a common part of the typical daily meals of the population.

Papaya was grown all over the island, and we would plant them outside our homes. It tasted wonderful and was a great item to put in a fruit blender if you were sick with malaria, as it kept you from dehydrating and kept all your body functions operating, and it tasted great.

Water was very hard to find on the island as it ran in the streams (about 10 to 15' wide from the mountain). We got our water by the road, and it is where the people bathed. This is pretty different from what we are used to, living in cities in countries like the United States. The first time my family came over, we went to town on Saturday, and there were all the ladies and kids bathing in the stream by our bridge. When they saw us, we stopped so they could get in the truck, but they had no clothes as they had been washed and hung on the bushes to dry and get the fly eggs. However, they still jumped in the truck without clothes and then put the clothes on afterward.

Cocoa and drying the cocoa was a business in the country. They would pick the yellow pods and break the pods, then empty out the seeds on a table to be dried. The tables were 60 to 90 feet wide and 200 to 300 long, with a steam-powered device to go up and down the table, turning the pods so they wouldn't rot or have fungus grow on them before they were dried. The cocoa grown on the island was some of the best in the world, as most of it was just placed on the ground and allowed to cure.

Coffee was not grown as a crop, but our living quarters were where the coffee plantation was located. So, when the trees bloomed, it seemed to be only one day, but the smell was so intensely sweet. By the end of the day, I was glad the flowering was over.

Electricity on the island was produced from a former Russian generator, and the people had power 3 to 4 days a week. Well, that wasn't guaranteed, too. You could get power half of the week if you were lucky. At most times, the power supply was incredibly inconsistent. Most foreign firms and embassies had their own setup for their electricity needs. Most of the foreign embassies had generators, but not all. One time, the generator that supplied the electricity to the President went down, so they called for the next maintenance person to come fix the generator, but when he got there, he couldn't fix it. So, he went to call the other guy, and the guard asked him where he was going. When he said the other maintenance person would finish the job, he was told that the other guy was in jail. And if he didn't want to be there, he better fix the generator so the machine got fixed. The problem with getting everyone electricity was that there was not enough electricity generated or even supply lines running to all the homes and businesses. Another problem was that there was no way to get everyone to pay their electric bill, as people would tie into other people's supplies and steal from one another.

Rain on the island was not consistent for the whole year, as it would stop from October to January. The malaria would never stop but lessen when the rain stopped. During the time of excess rain, it would send the malaria larvae to the streams. Here, they would be eaten by fish or go out to sea where they can't survive in the salt water.

Farming was the mainstay of most people in Equatorial Guinea. In some cases, the men did help their wives, but most did not. We helped with our D-9 Caterpillar to push back the large underbrush so the farmers could clean the small underbrush and then plant food crops for their families. The malanga and yuca roots were generally planted first, then the banana and plantain next, followed by the salad crop. Once the rains started, everything greened up and started to proliferate due to the rich soil. The weather was hot, and the people in the forest slept there with malaria, boas, cobras, and mambas. There were some gigantic lizards there, but what seemed interesting was that the people who slept there didn't get attacked.

POLITICAL SITUATION

In the intricate web of international relations, the interactions between major powers and smaller nations often shape the course of global politics and economics. China and the United States, as two of the world's leading superpowers, wield significant influence over smaller nations like Equatorial Guinea. This essay delves into the formal and complex relationships between these three entities, analyzing their interactions, economic ties, and geopolitical implications.

China's Expanding Influence

China's emergence as a global economic powerhouse has had far-reaching effects on nations worldwide, especially in Africa. Equatorial Guinea, a small West African country, has not been immune to China's expanding influence. China has played a key role in Equatorial Guinea's economic development through strategic investments and infrastructure projects. Chinese companies have been involved in constructing vital infrastructure such as roads, bridges, and energy facilities, bolstering the country's socio-economic landscape.

China's ambitious Belt and Road Initiative (BRI) has made a significant impact on Equatorial Guinea, boosting infrastructure development and strengthening economic ties between the two countries. This initiative has not only enhanced Equatorial Guinea's economic prospects but has also deepened its relationship with China, positioning the country as a key partner in China's broader global economic strategy.

Economic Partnership with the United States

While China has been a key player in Equatorial Guinea's development, the United States also maintains a significant economic presence in the nation. The U.S. has historically been a major importer of Equatorial Guinea's oil, a valuable natural resource that fuels the country's economy. American energy companies have played a pivotal role in the exploration and extraction of oil reserves, fostering economic cooperation between the two nations.

The triangular relationship between China, the United States, and Equatorial Guinea holds profound geopolitical implications. As China and the U.S. compete for global influence, smaller nations often find themselves navigating a delicate balance between these superpowers. Equatorial Guinea, like many other developing countries, must carefully manage its relationships with both nations to ensure economic stability and political autonomy.

In contrast to China's infrastructure-focused approach, the United States has engaged with Equatorial Guinea through diplomatic channels and development assistance programs. These initiatives aim to promote democratic governance, human rights, and economic diversification. U.S. aid has supported education, healthcare, and civil society development, fostering a positive relationship between the two nations beyond economic interests.

The Look Ahead

Despite the economic benefits gained from its relationships with China and the United States, Equatorial Guinea continues to face significant challenges. Balancing the interests of these global powers requires astute diplomacy and careful negotiation. Additionally, the nation must focus on sustainable development, diversifying its economy, and investing in education and healthcare to ensure long-term stability and prosperity.

The relationship between China, the United States, and Equatorial Guinea exemplifies the complexities of global diplomacy and economic interdependence. As these nations continue to interact within the framework of international relations, Equatorial Guinea stands at the crossroads, navigating a path that ensures its economic growth, political stability, and sovereignty. The dynamics of this triangular relationship underscore the challenges and opportunities faced by smaller nations in the ever-changing landscape of global politics and economics.

MA GIN WA
I LOVE YOU
(IN FANG)

$\approx \bullet \ll$

A great many people from the USA came to Malabo, but they did not work with, train, and understand the customs of the people or why the people had developed the ways of life they had. There were so numerous reasons that explained why the native people behaved in the way I have described throughout this book. One government took away the schools and entirely annihilated how you could succeed in life. Your father went to work, but you never saw him again, or you were told this person was bad or this person was good. When you were told something by the officials, you weren't allowed to think about it. You were to have complete faith in it and accept it as the fact that it portrayed to you.

They all had the same need food, water, electricity, health care, sewer, a street, or a job ($32 for a family of 6 for a month.) Mom and Dad plus the children worked the farm to get food and sell the extra in the market. Also, they want you to help them one way or the other. So, they would get close to you and take advantage of you if they got the tiniest chance. A 2" x 4" board or 4' x 8' piece of plywood to repair or build or sell for extra cash was a big deal in the country. A ride home in your vehicle would help them get whatever they could get or steal like a battery for a little or big piece of equipment. If you caught them, you would ask them to return it. But you knew to keep an extra eye on it because often, it was someone from the government requesting for equipment. And the person's family may be threatened if it is not obtained. It was up to you to choose what to do with them. For them, the consequences were terrible in all the possible ways. You could go one way and have them punished or fired, but you might make an enemy. And since you didn't have a weapon and ammo, you may want to take care where you went. You could always go to the ladies that offered the evening service, but that was not a good idea. We used to go to Gamba de Orea (golden shrimp) as the owner would run the ladies off, but if asked, these ladies would be available on demand. The new expats would be told how good the previous regime was and how bad the present government was. Sadly, they swallowed it hook, line, and sinker, as they never saw the people but played politics, thinking, they could move up the ladder.

I have seen people caned and blood running down their legs, but what they did wasn't repeated for a length of time.

Sadly, the love they have for you is not always good for you. So, you had to measure the love by what you could get help for. One guy came there and was asked for a report, so he turned it in. But since the minister didn't like it, he didn't get paid. However, he was hired to a position, where he could give things away so he did. Still, the truth is that he was never paid for his badly written report.

www.ingramcontent.com/pod-product-compliance
Lightning Source LLC
Chambersburg PA
CBHW040829120726
48005CB00012B/1555